The Beautiful Book for

DREAM SEEKERS

Laine Cunningham

The Beautiful Book for Dream Seekers

Published by Sun Dogs Creations
Changing the World One Book at a Time

Print ISBN: 9781946732712

Cover Design by Angel Leya

Copyright © 2018 and 2019 Laine Cunningham

All rights reserved. No part of this book may be reproduced in any form or by any means, electronic, mechanical, digital, photocopying or recording, except for the inclusion in a review, without permission in writing from the publisher.

The

BEAUTIFUL

BOOK

SERIES

Align Your Passion With Your Purpose

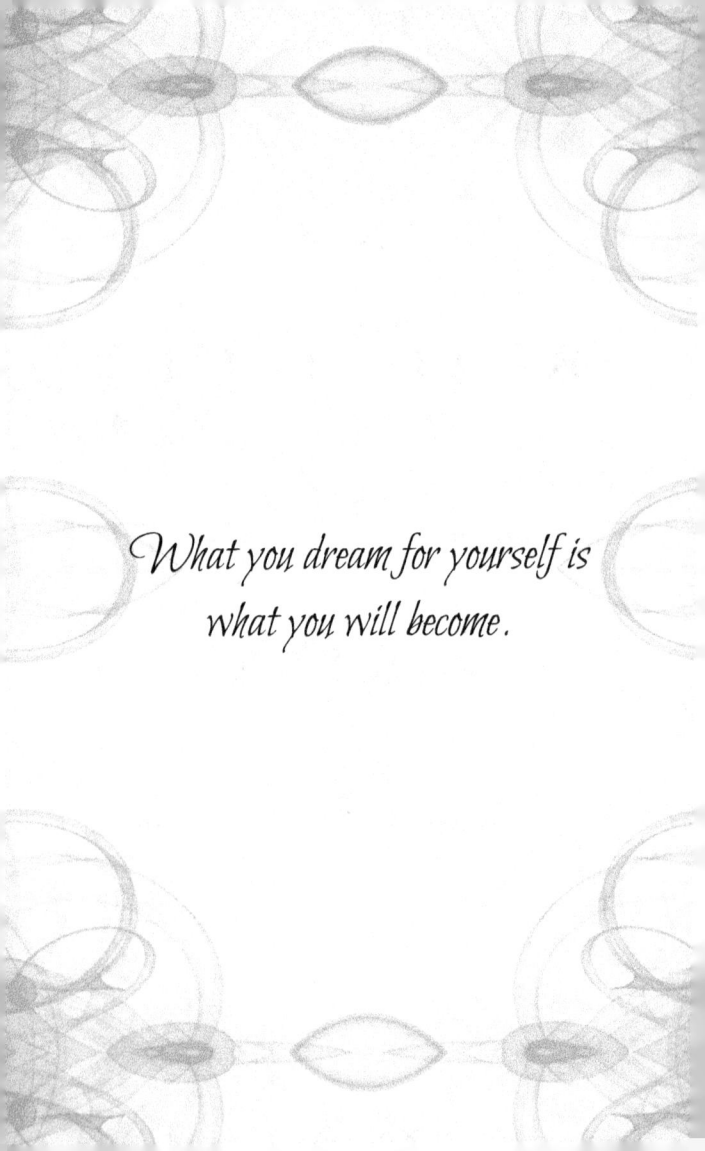

What you dream for yourself is what you will become.

A dreamer closes their eyes and opens their heart.

Your dreams are a premonition of the future you can create.

Harvest that which is abundant and wild.

*You already have
all that you need
to create
all that you desire.*

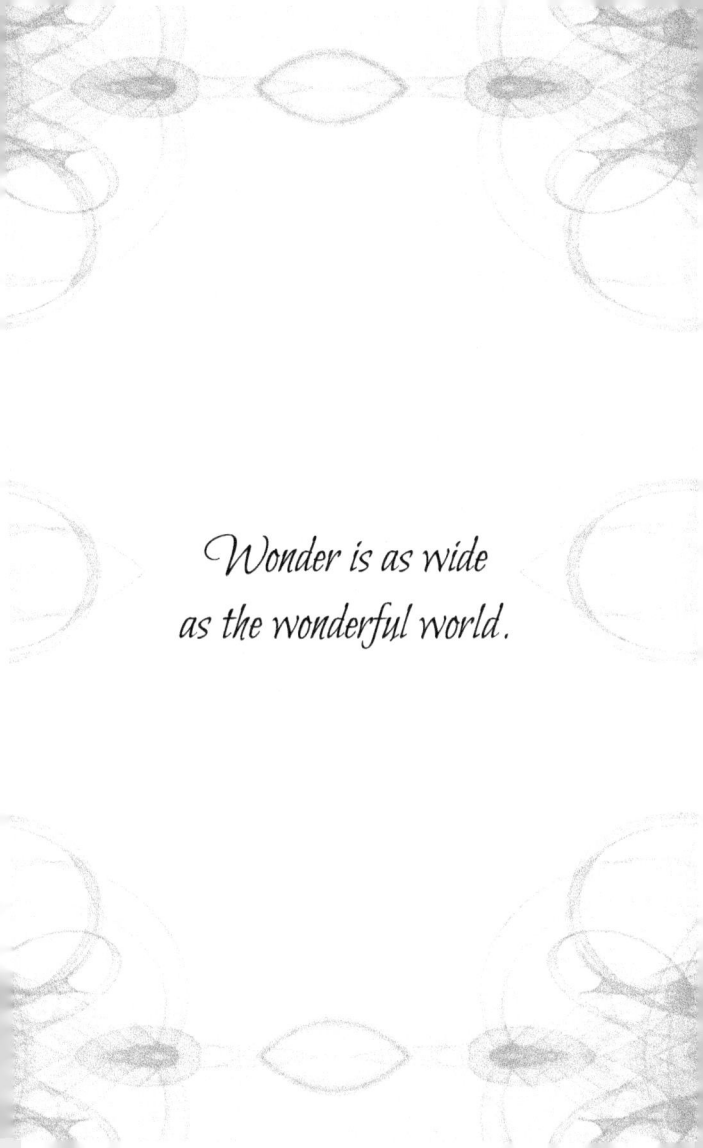

Wonder is as wide as the wonderful world.

*True magic
springs from your soul.*

Dreams are meant to be achieved.

A dream remembered is a dream fulfilled.

*Wonder fuels
all journeys.*

*To achieve flight,
lift yourself.*

*In the midst of silence,
hear your dream arrive.*

Expect the best to gain even more.

The sunflower is rooted, yet it turns toward the light.

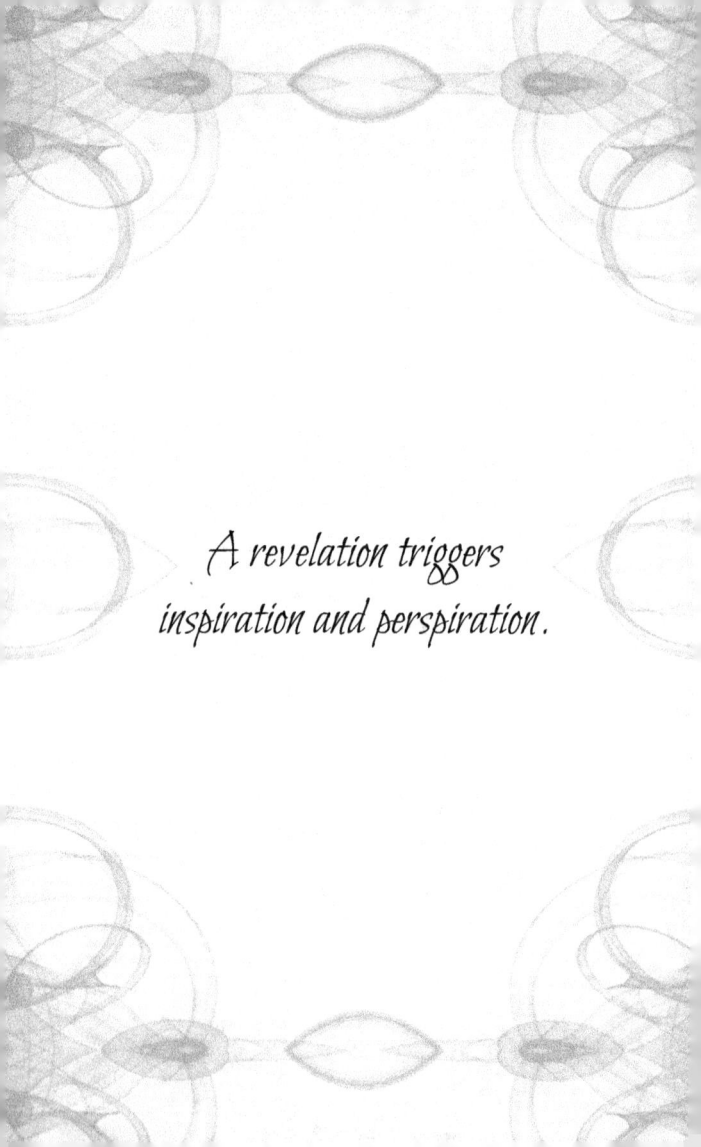

A revelation triggers inspiration and perspiration.

The boat that sails a lake can also sail an ocean.

Effort + Desire = Success

Value is measured by desire.

Inspiration is a starburst lighting the night.

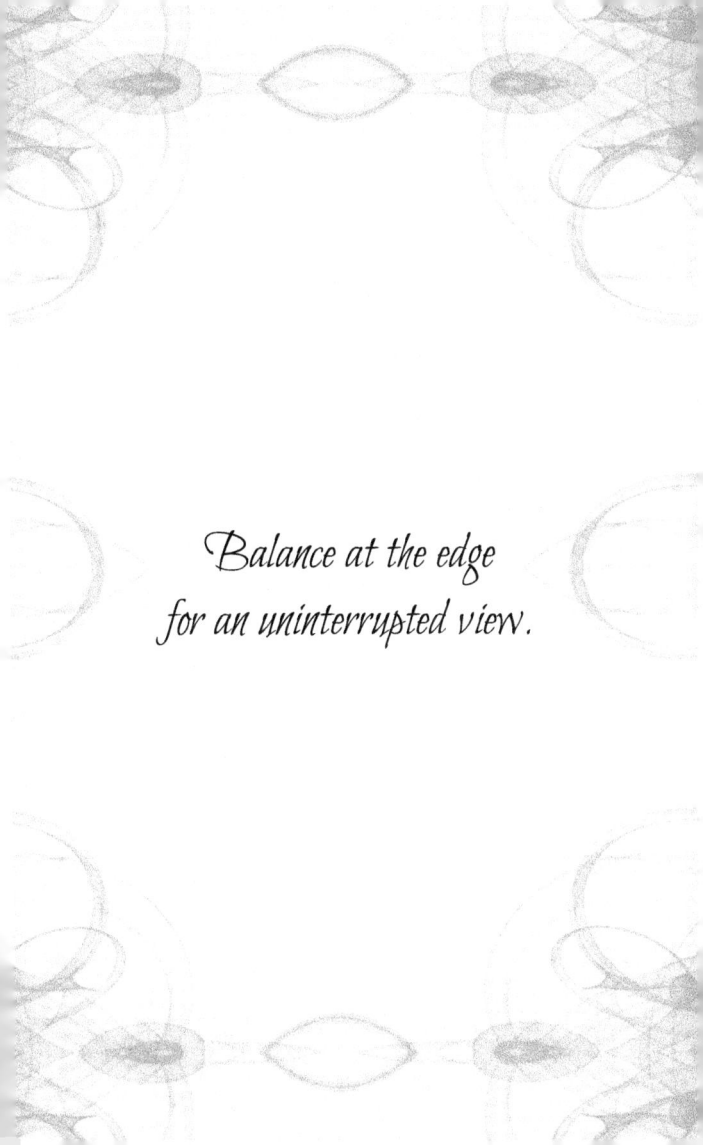

Balance at the edge
for an uninterrupted view.

*In the depths of passion,
you scale the greatest heights.*

*To see the light,
look up.*

One pinecone gives life to dozens of trees.

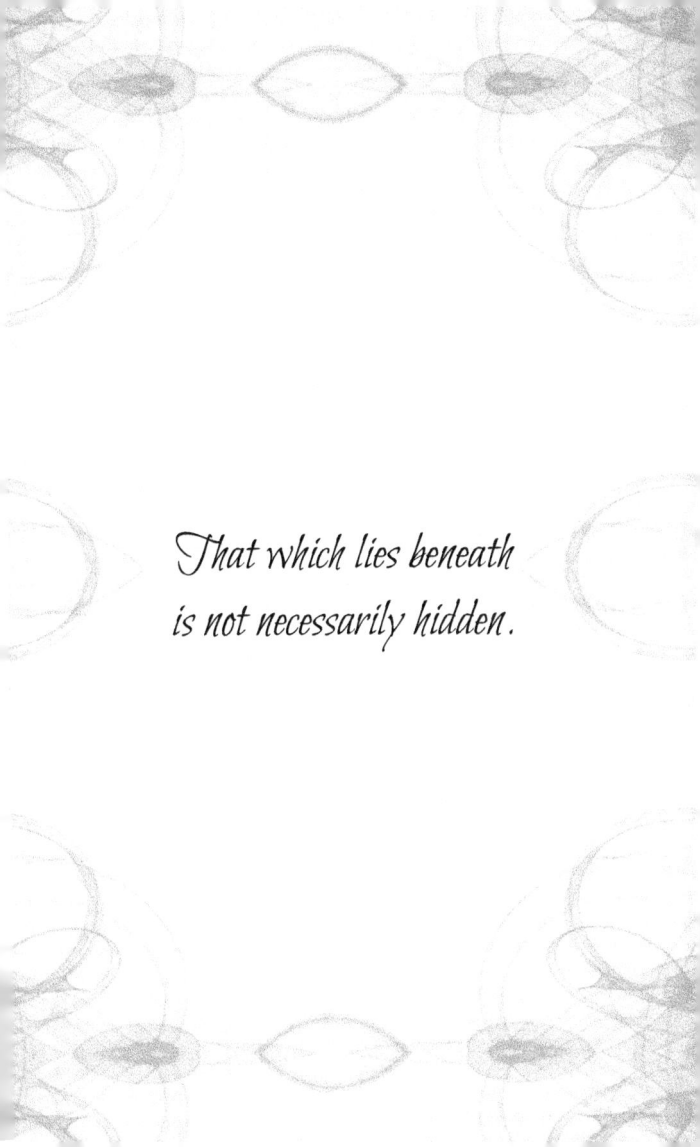

That which lies beneath is not necessarily hidden.

*Before a flower blooms,
it must form a bud.*

*The passage through
a dark tunnel
ends with an
eruption of light.*

Be like a migratory bird at home in many places.

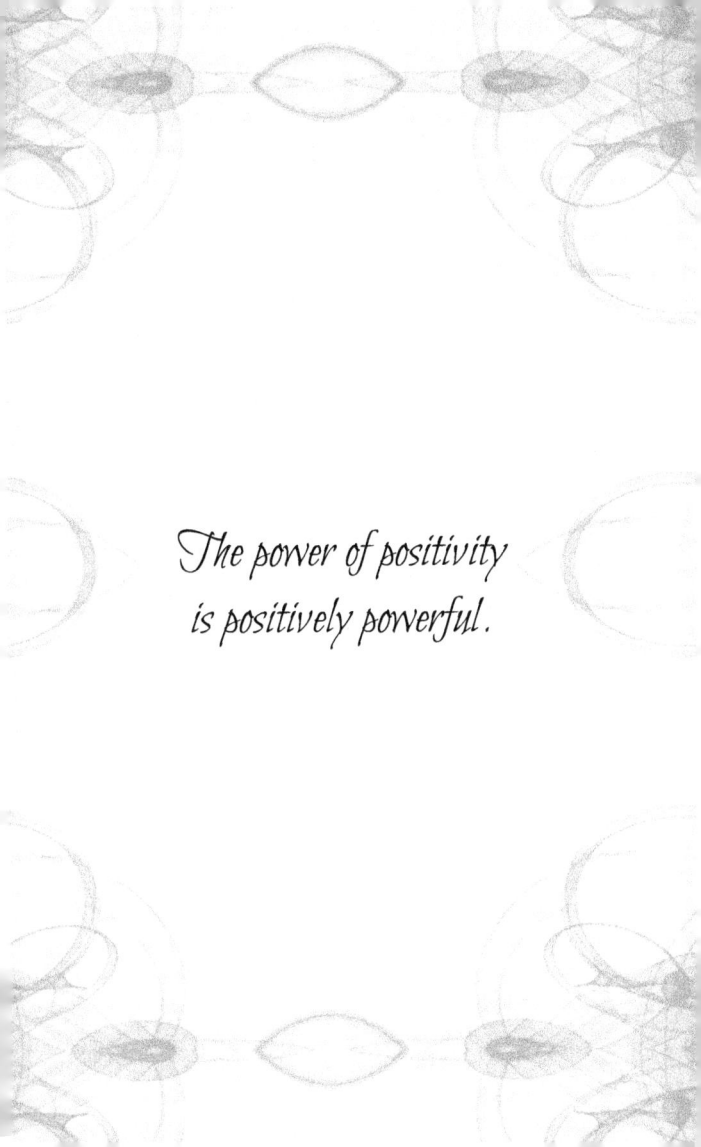

The power of positivity is positively powerful.

Fear not the dusk, for its silence brings peace.

Hope happens.

An accidental fall can become a soaring flight.

*Sometimes a single step
is bolder than a huge leap.*

*Mastery is built
one task at a time.*

*The molehill can be
as enriching
as the mountain.*

A steady pace carries you as far as a burst of speed.

Your universe constantly expands.

Harbor faith to create your safe harbor.

Even if you do not recognize the sound, your dreams are always chiming.

Dreams persist.

Prioritize your dreams to prioritize yourself.

The essence of your dreams is the essence of your happiness.

Sow your dreams like the seeds of wildflowers.

Feed your dreams and your dreams will feed your soul.

A valley can be more fertile than a mountaintop.

The unobstructed view gazes deep within.

Dreams are a resource that is truly unlimited.

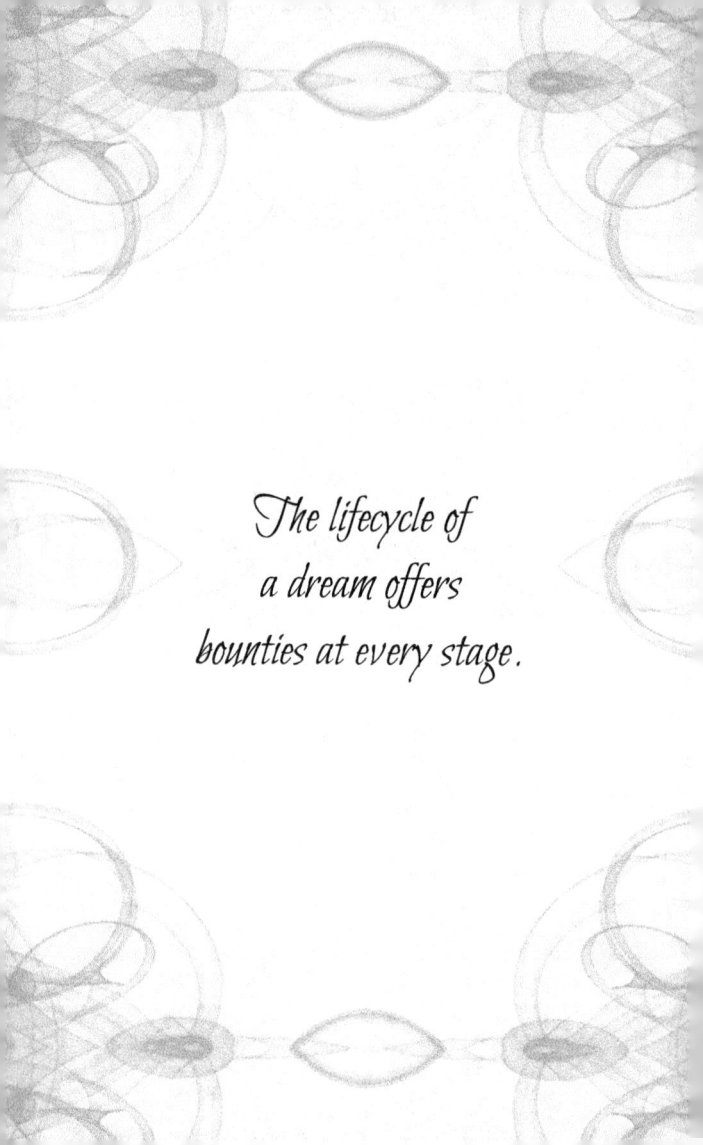

The lifecycle of a dream offers bounties at every stage.

*Chasing a dream
is as rewarding as
achieving it.*

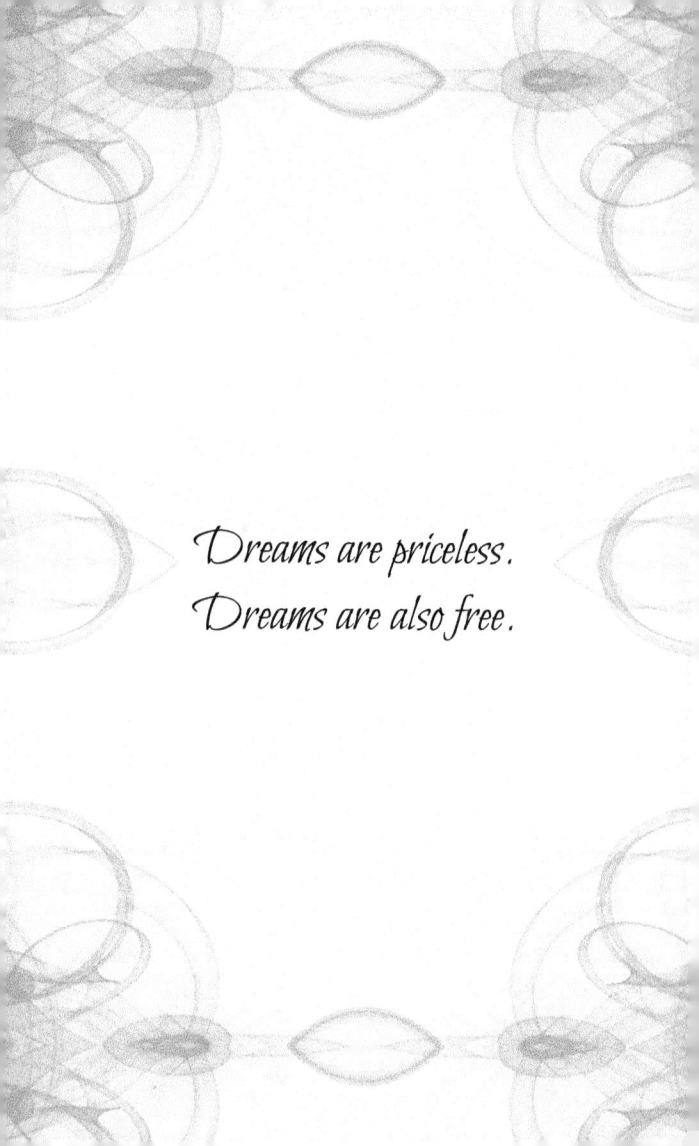

Dreams are priceless.
Dreams are also free.

Brilliant inventions spring from singular dreams.

*When you champion
your dreams,
you champion
many dreams.*

*Sail the rough sea
upon your buoyant dream.*

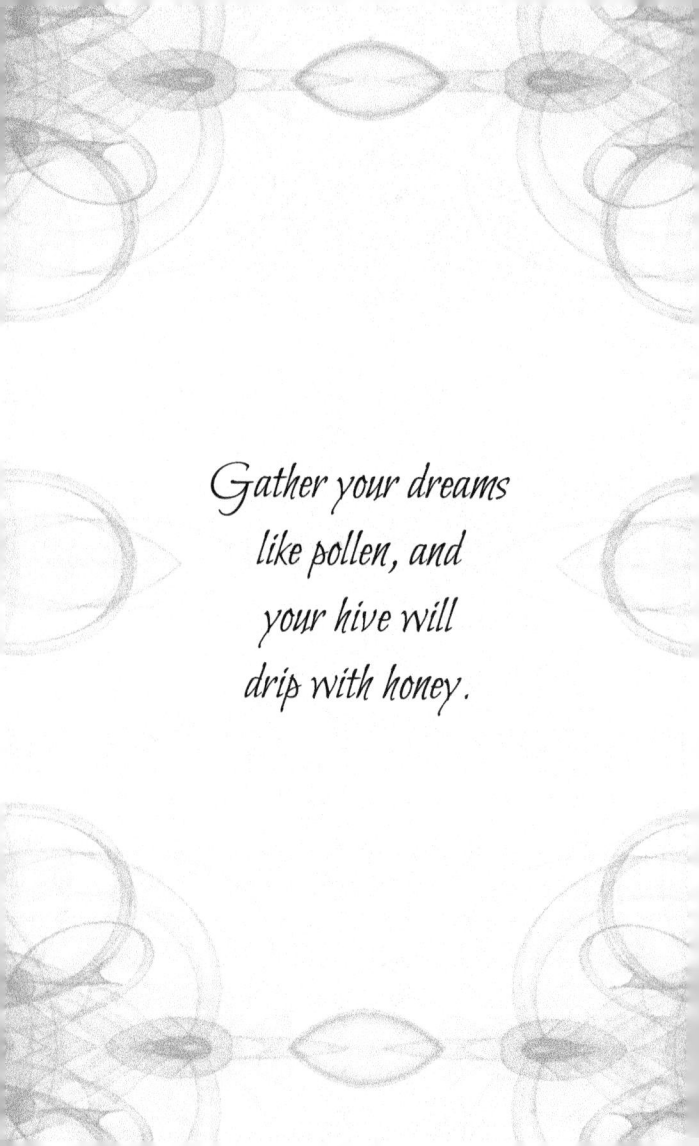

*Gather your dreams
like pollen, and
your hive will
drip with honey.*

*Dreams can be centered
on the self
without being selfish.*

A butterfly's erratic flight ends atop a flower.

*What you dream for yourself
is also your gift
to the world.*

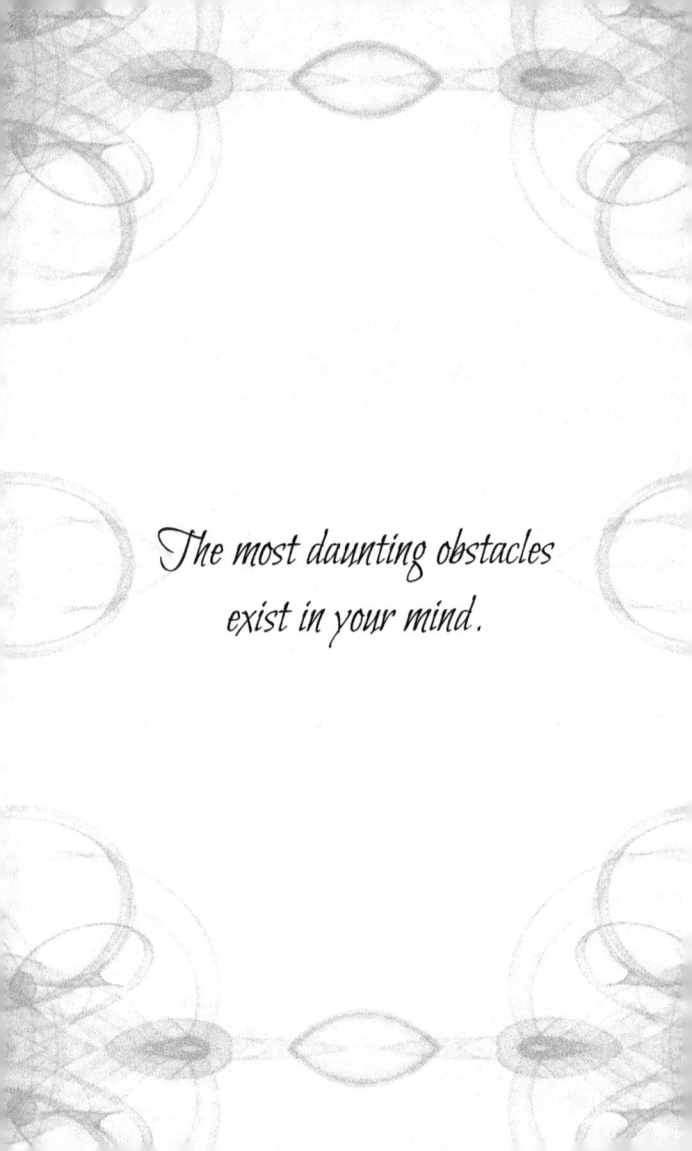

The most daunting obstacles exist in your mind.

*If the thought can arise
in your mind,
the dream can arise
in your life.*

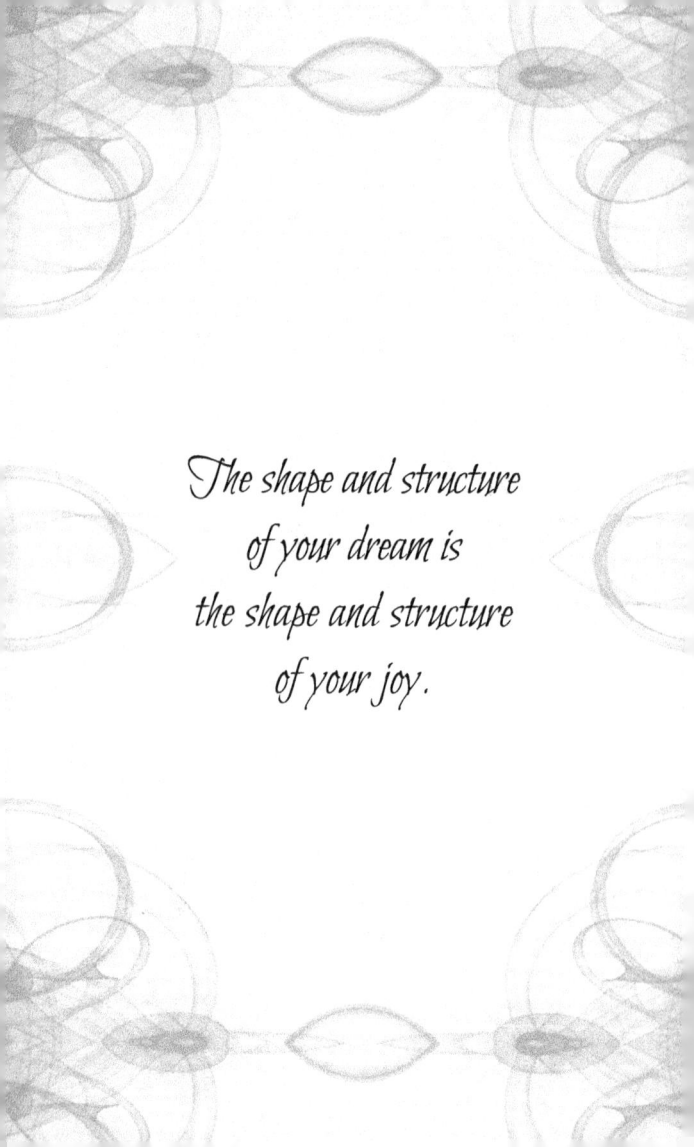

*The shape and structure
of your dream is
the shape and structure
of your joy.*

To discover the soul, consider the dreams.

Share your brightest dreams to brighten the world for others.

The stage play of your dream evolves in acts.

*Dreams unfold
into treasures untold.*

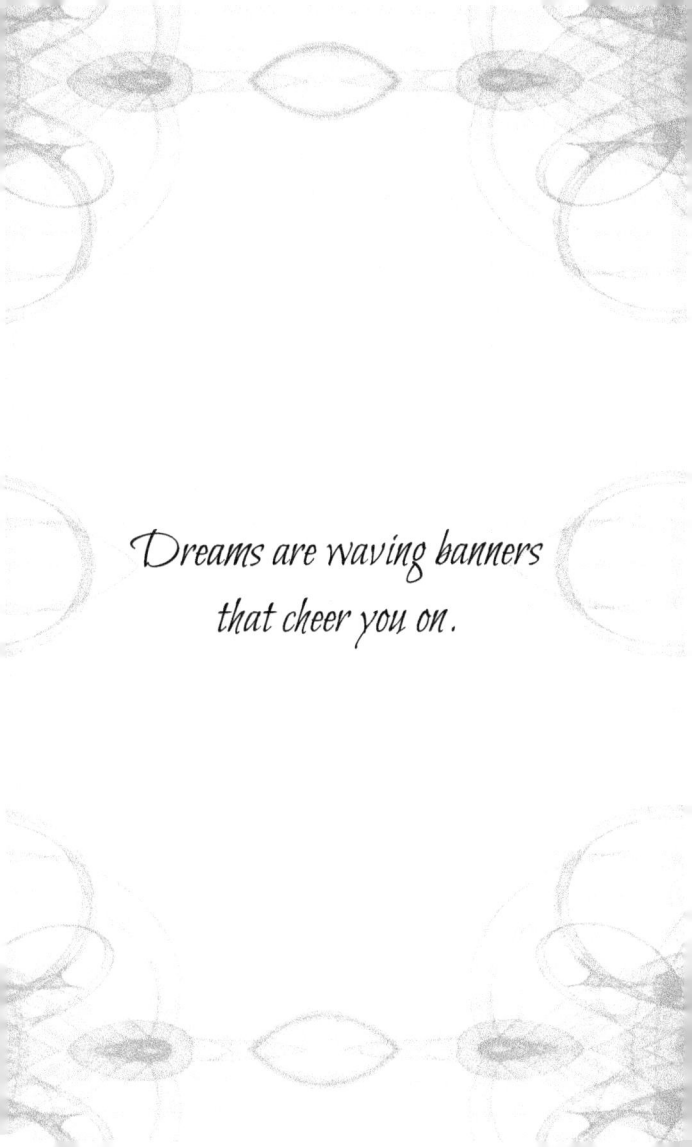

Dreams are waving banners
that cheer you on.

Dream seekers are also dream keepers.

*Everything that exists
in this world
exists to
support your goals.*

Novels by Laine Cunningham

The Family Made of Dust
Beloved
Reparation

Other Books by Laine Cunningham

Woman Alone: A Six-Month Journey Through the Australian Outback

On the Wallaby Track

Seven Sisters: Spiritual Messages from Aboriginal Australia

Writing While Female or Black or Gay

The Zen of Travel
The Zen of Gardening
Zen in the Stable
The Zen of Chocolate
The Zen of Dogs

The Wisdom of Puppies
The Wisdom of Babies
The Wisdom of Weddings

Bikes of Berlin
Necropolises of New Orleans I & II
Ruins of Rome I & II
Ancients of Assisi I & II
Panoramas of Portugal
Nuances of New York
Glimpses of Germany
Impressions of Italy
Altitudes of the Alps
Knights Through the Ages
Coast of California
Utopia of the Unicorn
Flourishes of France
Portraits of Paris
Tableaus of Tbilisi
Grandeur in the Republic of Georgia

The Beautiful Book of Questions
The Beautiful Book for Dream Seekers
The Beautiful Book for Rebels
The Beautiful Book for Women
The Beautiful Book for Lovers

www.ingramcontent.com/pod-product-compliance
Lightning Source LLC
Chambersburg PA
CBHW070104120526
44588CB00034B/2245